HUMAN LOVE

human
love

DOREEN GILDROY

THE UNIVERSITY OF CHICAGO PRESS
Chicago and London

DOREEN GILDROY is the author of *The Little Field of Self*, which
won the John C. Zacharis First Book Award of *Ploughshares* maga-
zine. She lives in Irvine, California.

The University of Chicago Press, Chicago 60637
The University of Chicago Press, Ltd., London
© 2005 by The University of Chicago
All rights reserved. Published 2005
Printed in the United States of America

14 13 12 11 10 09 08 07   2 3 4 5

ISBN: 0-226-29330-0   (paper)

Library of Congress Cataloging-in-Publication Data

Gildroy, Doreen.
  Human love / Doreen Gildroy.
    p. cm. — (Phoenix poets)
  ISBN 0-226-29330-0 (alk. paper)
  I. Title. II. Series.
  PS3607.I43H86 2005
  811'.6—dc22

                                    2005016546

for Michael

and for Emily

*We have found, not the thing itself, but where it is
to be sought; and that will suffice to give us a point
from which a fresh start may be undertaken. . . .*

*. . . both sought that it may be found, and found that it
may be sought; still sought that the finding may be
sweeter, still found that the seeking may be more
eager.*

—S T . A U G U S T I N E , *Later Works*

Contents

Acknowledgments

Grateful acknowledgment is made to the following publications in which these poems first appeared:

American Poetry Review: "Gallery of My Life," "Luminaries," "Open to the Sky," "Transit," and "Unmitigated Hue"

Slate: "Human Love"

TriQuarterly: "Vademecum," "Visitation," and "Visual Binary"

N O T E :

This book is indebted to Vitruvius's *The Ten Books on Architecture*. "Open to the Sky," "Clearstock," and "Diagram of the Winds" use architectural terminology as metaphor.

I

Prolusion

This is my kitchen.
I looked around.

You think I would have noticed before
that it was safe.

(I started to feel.)

What I wanted first
was color.

I intended terra-cotta,
but the paint turned
twice as vibrant:
true orange.

(And then I became used to
boldness.)

Human Love

When the child wouldn't come
into existence
what was I to do?
I knew it in a different way, then.

He said he had never heard
these stories
before we began, didn't care—
but now in his grief
they seemed everywhere.

        *

I was missing you,
and then the dove.

Singly—not in a pair—
in his usual place.

I watched him
on the garden wall,
thought the absence
of the other.

Whatever the reason,
I took it to

remind me of myself
and what I was missing.

It flew up
in the face of
all my instinct,
my raw animal comfort.

       *

His was a tender embrace.

There was nothing going on
around it,

no fury
driving me on.

In spite of the pain
I was offering something.

Some days this seems
everything I understand.

Gallery of My Life

In the gallery
I listen to a story.
What the open space is for—
always that small pressure.

If I need to go to bed,
is it illness, or mercy?

I overheard a woman say,
"It didn't matter that . . ."

                    *

Outside,
I watched the people talking.

"He was always
excited about everything.
That's what was nice about him."

Quiet in a chair,
reading the ancient texts.

I decided to try human guides.

I wanted someone who says,
This is a world,
I like to see it.

        *

A vital force.

I decided not to talk about it
anymore,
but still pursue.

Perhaps I will wake up
further along, on another path
completely.

        *

For a long time
I couldn't discard
the papers,
reading lists,
classics
vast and dense.

Where had I been before?

Far stronger, far brighter for me
this indication,
like a star.

I must be a strange being by now.

My God,

it took me many years
to get here.

> *And then we began to speak.*

Exposing my sense of time
as utterly limited.

> *Because time is what's between us.*

I know nothing,
not even Christ.

> *I wish I had learned—*
> *so I'm starting now.*

Not human form—
which to me, my heart, would
not be recognizable.

> *There was a place on earth*
> *that corresponded.*

I carried its vestiges—
always carried your
traces.

Unmitigated Hue

Oh wild, elegant
landscape—
everchanging
hailstorm, light.

What will be my book? the many books.
Who will be my guide?

*

After so many years
the absolute scared me.
I remembered it, certainly—
as if over me

I felt the weight of it.

*

Sitting by the irrigation pond
somewhere in Idaho,
I grew weary of my myth of childhood.

The list of names I read, of which
I want to replace
one with our child,

an ancient name made
vital.

*

Without signs (the usual)
this naming was difficult.

There's really nothing in the room.
(I've cleaned everything out.)

The air
cool today.
(Nothing left in the house.)

I'd forgotten my powers.

In the morning
I could say anything.

Vademecum

We were going to go
to the museum—
looking, studying.

It was just around the corner.

But we decided
to sit in *Rita Flora*
in the balmy breeze
and eat cake.

The afternoon had all gone so slowly.
I was happy with him—
and felt it,
continually.

My soul is tired, I say.
And why it comes out
that way, I don't know.

I could not figure it.
Today, simply stopped
requesting to know.

We'll wander around
and the day will go on—

and so will I—
and I'll reach for nothing

that doesn't touch me,
doesn't present itself

inquisitive of me.

Tables and Chairs

I'm on the table again,
and the new doctor probes.
Tables and chairs,
they are my residences.
Heaven on earth?
I keep a telescope in my closet.
Where I place the stars?
The birds eternal,
catching us, calling
their redirection.
Ten o'clock—and I remember
sitting in a room . . .
My brain's good to me,
keeps things.
Right place, perfect place, and
ease.
The eldress sits
in the shaker chair.
It is a life. Her life.
Not ashamed to be as she is.

II

Returning to my father's house—
in a dream

in my great disappointment
I've come looking for him

in chaos, in citizens' revolt

roaming foreign streets,
and the snow is everywhere.

He's been dead almost ten years,
and he's so happy to see me.

In a dream he once told me "Separate."
Once, a dream of light

to not return to the fallen city.

Being Marked, Showing Symptoms

What's the purpose of all of this
when you know I couldn't possibly
understand?
You know, I will ask what I will ask.
It's your answer
I've come to find out—that,
and how far
I'm actually
willing to go.

Vitruvius says
there is nothing wrong
with building a house.

Harmony and proportion.
There began to be gifts of music.

I mixed the bone meal
in the new soil,
and kneaded the earth.
I plan to put
anything down.

For too long
the perfect landscape
has kept me waiting,

I no longer expected it—
but I did expect
something.

I told myself
I am not sick,
just barren.

And in the world
there *were* women with children
though they weren't mine.

For seven years I waited—
and each year
my love for him increased,
and each night
I made a newer vision of you and
what I would call you
when we had finished
taking all the grief out of our bodies
knowing that that perhaps
might be your only purpose.

Visitation

I don't know why I was there.
The walls were very grey,
a great box.
Their skin was translucent,
had something of the child to it.
I saw them, at first, only
in glimpses
out of the side of my eyes
so that I had to question.
It was terror, no great virtue in me,
that made me
do what was necessary.
What correspondence to body?
This was form.
The only stipulation
is that I choose it
and thereby acquire judgment
through desire.
There was something
besides me.
It moved me,
not because it rescued me
from any immediate predicament
(this I was not to know)—
but because it was
a thing of unknown beauty.

This was the new image
placed in my mind.
The way they moved—
I had to look—and
they were interested.

Reconnaissance

First, I had to allow it—
before I could change it.

I would dare;
daring is what I had
to do first.

The past presented a guide,
my younger self,
not to torture, but to tell:

Go out and look at the same tree, she said.
(I would not see the same thing.)

From the other side, and forward.
Two versions before me.

I don't know how to get there, I said.
Could the paradise be so subtly found?

Walking through the door
I could now pass both ways.

Visual Binary

Fear was the invisible field
that separated them:

The beasts, the elders;
the old view of the lovers,
the old landscape.
Who wouldn't be
bewildered?
(The sulphur mud pools . . .)

I was speaking to you
and then I understood
my myth of childhood.

The bandages covered my face
so I couldn't see
what was taking place.
When the bandages came off
my mother gave me
all the books I wanted.

      *

Subject to despair—
I am not all-
conquering.

Utterly cold,
under attack.

Why not be
an animal,
unblamed?

Painful, I won't deny.

To put the question on, and
behave as if: beautiful dress.

                    *

I remember always
I can't live this life
and another.

Just as vibrant,
just as myself.

The animals were
coming around, coming out:
buffalo, moose, and elk—
and the blue heron.
The geysers
would not stop.

I could sit on a hill
and watch.

The children were blinking.

Transit

It's a tempting thought—
and quick to practice.

It was always that thought
I went back to
in my weakness,
so that I came
no longer to believe it.

Weren't there other postulates
that wanted to appear?

I started that day
with the sketch of angels
on my wall—
Raphael's
chalcographie.

Cooking in the kitchen,
I looked out the window
and the four trees rose up
green and circular,
the leaves
balanced on the thin
shoot of

pale bark.
Behind them, more trees.

My exile saved me.
I learned to speak myself
out of what was denied me.

I went to bed last night thinking
Maybe this was right . . .

The night sky was pink.
1 a.m. and Leonid
passing through its thirty-six years
in meteoric flight . . .

so I went to sleep
and thought of it all

above, going on—

I was walking into the future.

I remember my mother painting the landscape,
cutting the flowers, in relief, with her
palette knife.

I will not be afraid of it.
I will not hate it.

If the stars
are to be ignored
why such (power and) light—

purely in the world?

As Vitruvius to the Divine
Intelligence

What could I build for you?
My slot of window, my geometric sphere . . .
(what I know of mechanics and sundials).
I could see.
The mind, fire
to the touch of body.
(How I understand the temple.)
Oh, the height of the face itself!
What will be my measure—
for land and water?
How beautiful to lay it out.
The doors: this one looks better,
but this one is strength.
What good is my love
without manifestations?
There would be errors
of pronunciation.
A little hope.

Open to the Sky

He was the first thing I saw
when I woke up.
His face, looking intently . . .
then the burnt sienna
of his shirt
flooding the drab recovery room.

Two white roses,
they are the only things I have
from the outside.
The refined and rarefied air
that comes from green things,
image distinct.

I have had to move slowly today—
deference to the body.
And the little Japanese bird
sings from the postcard
on the dresser.

I was imagining a robe.
I was moving like a woman moves.

The old idea was mattering
less.

Everything I normally
took from habit
repulsed me.
I was interested in taste,
and what I might like now.
I felt—a clean palate.

I was beginning to learn something
about myself, about
how I wanted to move through
the world

so I wouldn't miss it—
so I wouldn't have to make
others suffer so.

Reprieve

The body held
perfectly still, almost forgotten,
and I could question—
most wildly.

That something good
comes after disappointment, and
the good, now, to be able
to bear the latter . . . ?

A friend says
do nothing today—
do nothing all week.
Stay in your robe;
whatever you feel like
in your house.

This my capacity, this:
my receptacle of anger.

That's the broken heart—
I recognize it,
but can't help myself.

What if I quit trying?

What would you say then?

Miniature

He would like to make something
in the morning.

A figure, sitting—
at the
constant table.

My husband
is working away.
In spite of doubt and fear,

he's working away.

The high window—
with its
verdigris pane,

the violet light.

L u m i n a r i e s

I

It wasn't suffering
exactly, no, not quite vulnerability—
more the registering
on his face—of
all of it:
everything he could possibly give.

To know, to be known . . .

Mirror of my body, mirror
of this night.

II

Lovely to walk on the beach,
under the late
grey winter sky

and on to the grand hotel—
all Hollywood and Wizard-of-Oz lights.

We stare at the great ceiling above us.

My mentor, my friend—
he was asking me
about my life.

The guide of work, the guide of
getting on with it,
the guide of looking
at the world.
Blue eyed.

III

It's not that
I haven't felt this before—
this just more chaotic,
melodramatic.

Depression is
flat-lined,
very calmly
not wanting—not wanting
to get out of bed.

Dream of a spider, dream
of a bug. Under our dresser—
I'm trying to kill it. I dream—
Egyptian woman
with wings—
talking to me.

I'm chasing her;
she's talking, and I'm following.

Fountain

I contain all the emotions.
Why pretend I don't?

Fountain of youth, fountain of the
untold . . .

I'm cleansing the water,
flowing freely.

Take me as your symbol.
What have you got to fear?

Be bold, as you step over.
(You have studied me enough.)

See how the little fish swim
into all perpetuity?

III

Bonsai

It's a little tree,
yet sturdy—
and strangely forceful

though how can it contend
with the larger trees
that need so little? that take so much?

One simple thing.
Why do I compare?

Cut, shaped, formed.
What compels?

This is how I am,
this is how I will be.

I attend: little scissor;
pan of water—

quietly breaking
the brittle ends,
trimming
all waywardness.
A continual

looking for
the green.

So restful, so confirming,
the colored pebbles
scattered
on the moist black earth.
The focus; the stones.

You're in a different season.

Entry

> *For one is not disposed to contemplation*
> *which leads to mental elevation unless*
> *one be with Daniel a man of desires.*
>
> —BONAVENTURE

A doorway, or gate
between the columns?

I could perceive it;
I looked for it.

It was sunny,
and I was in shade.

I felt little pain.

       *

That the map
is not the country itself
everybody knows.

Then the world
grew out of focus for me;

I felt a small body
in need of much care,
monitored—

whose only task
was to subject itself
and not die,
take in the necessary, trusting.

I could not predict.
I knew not how I would grow.

      *

I let the meditations
move

where they would go—
having done all I could think of.

What was I meditating on?

On the nature of.

This is how I felt most,
how I would go at it:
I think of the story,
and for me it changes.

      *

In the dream
the baby woke.

I liked that it would be
good and bad.
I looked forward to its imperfections,

its glories—
what it would seek,
and how it would
speak to that.

And it would speak to me.
And there would be exchange.

The Center of the Earth, Unseen

You are for the living.
I so wanted to live.
I so want the child to live.

Maybe I've been changed by now.
The good could whisper, and I let it.

Lying in the dark,
I looked up, once again

as in the little field
when I was a girl.

I remembered the strangeness
of the ginkgo leaves:
and sometimes a poppy
(evident, present)—but the mind
would pursue the chosen.

I can't believe I wouldn't
recognize

the scene, a perfect image of stillness.
It being in the right order.

Paints, Medicines

To illuminate
the book,
the child.

On the eleventh day,
he must give me the injections, too.

The mere dark not evil—
you have given us
a certain fluency.

*

My mother had been painting flowers
and I had been watching.

How the tubes
became the paint.
How the color
contained the story—
even the subtle shades.

Study of the jars
on the shelf.

Here is the mixture.
And it must be
a re-creation.

       *

The animals must be like us—
in their quiverings.
(I don't always know what they will do.)

When he cracks the glass ampule
open, I can hear it
all the way down the hall.

And the body will follow
with its unstoppable list. . . .

One ampule must be mixed
through the sixth;
the fine powder,
into solution.

       *

The child
a vision, but—
even in your mind?
Weren't even you
overwhelmed
by the desire
(to look into another being)?

And I've come to expect this vision.
I've come to call upon expecting.

*

How do the human things get mixed in?

Not propulsively,
not forward or upward—
and I've been so meticulous,
tried so hard to be
the transforming agent.

And then the result becomes
different than I thought—
and the thought changes,
even the color of what I was looking for.

Diffusion

How I longed for the earth,
outside—plants, animals;
minerals, stones.
The shape of the room
(my confinement)—
rectangular, triangular.
Here one angle,
then another. How
the water glass circles
from the bottom up . . .
On the high wall—
my ever slight
movement.
How distorted my mind, saturated—
and in the sleepless night,
what has taken place?
Density, intensity.
Constant, as if alive.
Pain has a beginning, a middle, and an end, she said.
A trace of white through the slate blinds.
I reach for the bowl of black grapes.
Sepia near the earth, sometimes
purple sky.

Artificial Paradises

I

There was always time to talk
(in my mind's thought).

Choose the spouse, not the
philosopher.

II

As long as the ritual would allow
the body
to make its meandering trail . . .

Did I ever know
I could feel so weak?

If I just stayed here
and didn't move.

Maybe I'm not ready for the gift.

III

Not the same world, clearly.
Darkness, called into it by desire:
fiery.

As much as the idea wanted
to rise above
the flesh, it was human.

Joy mingling demise—
(I'm not blind).
That the two are here present
seemed important to know.

IV

This was my paradise:
A moment, any second: refuge.

Oh—so much larger than I had dreamed
when I went exploring.
The body's shedding,
sheer terror to the skin.

It's not pretty, always:
the soul's raw garment.

V

My companion, a light
that led me.

He felt things
I couldn't feel.
He became
what he could not
be before.

I was no longer allowed to walk around the same.
How could the prayer be the same?

VI

At times when I was allowed to stand
I would look out the blinds
at the tiny cactus sprouting

three shades
(I didn't know
existed till now)—

a vibrant orange
opening their flowers.

And the drive, the desire,
its calling almost unbearable to me.

I felt I couldn't get there.
(In the extreme time.)
Here is the place I could tell.
All unglorious.

Did you think it would be ceasing?

Clearstock

It's what I've always wanted to know.

> *Trees vary and are unalike*
> *in their qualities.*

How would I fill the book?

> *Is it natural that they*
> *should be alike?*

The story changes.

> *I am changed by it.*

The part which is nearest to the earth . . .

> *Cut it at the core.*

Four pieces, joiner's work.

It's what I've understood about you.

If I were waiting for the world.
If I were waiting for . . .
what would happen to the world?

The world for me.

IV

In Illo Tempore

Without symmetry and proportion there can
be no principles in the design of any temple;
that is, no precise relation between its
members, as in the case of a well shaped man.
—V I T R U V I U S , *The Ten Books on Architecture*

The idea I had had,
the judgments—
systems of the world . . .

It's its own world—
what happened there.

There was nothing I wanted to read.

The book would finish itself,
in the forming.

*

On the screen
the four beings move
in their animal form—

some fragile, some reaching
into consciousness—
until it is time . . .

What was that idea?
Never really the divine, never really
the self . . .

Yet, what does the body know?

A body formed for one child.

*

I understood depth.
(I don't know
all of depth yet.)

Our grief is confusing.
There is suffering.

There are greys and blacks here—
looking for the lightness.

Conjoined—
the colored spectrum shows

their little lives, still alive . . .

and this is the nature of their life,
the doctor says:
that it will be short.

*

The doctor says this is what the body
does
(though now we see it):

absorb quietly,
with little pain—even the seemingly
perfectly formed.

The numbers, the beings.

The body is reaching the limit,
knowing not to push on,
and it does this—
mostly in secret.

Life that wants to live,
that is helped along

(its perfect proportion)—

reflects the facial bones,
the jaw line;
the arms moving, and
open.

*

Not of my hand.

There is the life
and death
of ideas—

where one image
must be replaced
by another.

I began to wake up very early.

Refuge from myself,
forever scrutinizing.

I began enjoying being human.

This was innocence for me.

A Picture Like the Sun

The choice between
a harsh day and a gentle one . . .

I was thinking of the child.

I didn't want to save it,
or spare it, or
think I could—
but to give it something,
some particular vision.

Night clouds, trees . . .

Letting it come to me
like the little birds.

I was up
and tending the plants
for the first time.

Out the kitchen window, in the garden—
how balmy the air.
How still.

I used to like the room
dark, but now

like the sun.
How else would I
have come to
see it?

All the colors lined up
above the fierce green.

Imperfect Awe

Everywhere, evident—
the house.

The pace of my life.

I woke up in the clean white sheets,
in the white room.
Perhaps I am naive
(what one has to do!)
following.

Walking where I live,
I was feeling very tender—

what I went through with him . . .

the leaves have come out on the apricot tree.

I was afraid the quiet would leave me,
but it is adamant —
as the creatures have:
a view and a voice.

I remember reading
the lines of streets
as a little girl.

The world is larger
because we have lived into it.

Field Work

Infinity of Space is like a Painters Table,
prepared for the Ground and feild of those
colors that are to be laid theron . . . As the Table
is infinit so are the pictures.
                              —T R A H E R N E, from *Centuries 5-5*

When I finally understood I was suffering,
then you said—No more suffering.

What sets it in motion? *Time.*

Time needs to rest.

> *

At the oldest vet school, near Paris,
they show the horses' hocks
on the sonogram.

How nimble the doctors are,
handling the animals—
which appear innocent,
trusting.

A woman cradles a small tiger—
(which I didn't think possible.)

> *

All the families here
in this beachtown,
this holiday weekend—
breakfasting on the hill.

One child colors,
another—a little girl
in leopard pants
listens to her mother's plaintive
"just one bite."

The characters that were useful. The ones that
presented themselves.

I could expose it, or overexpose it; it would

come out a different picture—
what would become clear.

I think of a friend's circular postcard.

"In search of something nice to think about," he says.
"I am just about to leave to Crete and Athens."

*

Reading about the battle of the world, of paradise.
Of angels, and Satan—and all those trees!

What is your cedar, pine, and fir?
And the triumphant palm . . .

The books said, I said.

Today is the day.

On the table I dreamt.
How will she see the city?
The hill?

I gave all my attention

because the doctor said
it would protect her
if I tried not to move.

                    *

In Pascal's cafe,
morning—

and I watch through the pane-glass windows
how the women scurry
to place the full roses.

He asks me
if I am anxious,
but we are out today
and I feel only relief at that.

He reads the newspaper
and writes.

Today—thinking about the roses,

how he took on the job of caring for them—
came to love them—
and what did he know of roses!

How I would move the delicate ones

from the backyard
to the front
with the others of their kind—

and do something utterly different
in the backdrop.

I'd have to learn as I went along.

Bring them into the world, I thought.

It Is the Beginning

I had a visitor.

And what did the visitor say?

You were secretive, and luminous . . .
You said, Consider the enterprise.

And was it love?

You said, What is
the repeated gesture?

And did you love?

A gorgeous creature—
with blazing eyes.

Strange Flowers

I was never content
with the names of things, but
I could remember
in vivid detail: the motion,
the scent,
what I was thinking.
The strange flowers . . .
the first time we were walking
in the landscape—
and you were new to me.
I wanted to know what they were
and for that reason
I sat and watched them,
for a long time.
I always felt—
being in their presence—
the leaves were nothing,
but the long green stalk
would grow and grow
so singular
before the effulgence
of petal after purple petal.
I would seek them out
always with a sense of reverie—
and when people would ask me
what I called them

I never felt shame
not knowing.
This is why I liked having
them in our garden.
(Now I see them everywhere.)

Diagram of the Winds

et ex mente tota

sum presantialiter

and from my whole mind

I am face to face